SELECTED ART SONGS

OF

HELEN C. CRANE

MEDIUM VOICE

with piano accompaniment

BOOK TWO

Bernard R. Crane

Editor

ISBN 978-1-735-8882-8-6
BISAC: MUS037110
LOC Classification: M6 – 175.5

all pieces copyrighted under the title Collected Vocal Music of Helen C. Crane - Book I
©2020 Bernard R. Crane
ASCAP

Helen C. Crane in her mid 20's (c. 1890)
enhanced photograph of Helen C. Crane as pictured in the publication
"The Music Monitor" July. 1919 – Vol. VIII, No. 10

DAYS OF DISCOVERY

Just a few minutes of spare time and a bit of curiosity is all that it took to launch myself on a quest that has now encompassed the last two years. Thanks to the wonders of the digital age more and more information is accumulated in smaller and smaller formats, occupying less and less space. Where once the entire floor of an office building was necessary to house one computer, now an entire library of reading material can be stored on a device not much larger than a little finger. One of the results of this every burgeoning ability to collect, store, and share materials is a unique collective enterprise known as International Music Score Library Project or IMSLP, present online at www.imslp.org . With the cooperation of individuals, schools and universities, through the pooling of resources we have reached a point where a significant portion of published music that is no longer copyright, is now available. In light of this rich source which I have used many times in the past, and being a composer myself, with degrees from Eastman and the San Francisco Conservatory, I was curious if there were any other CRANE's listed on IMSLP website. I did find five: Adam Crane, a gentleman who seems to have been more of a performer or teacher than a composer: his one page inclusion was "NiffTShift" some sort of performance method for shifting positions on a stringed instrument. Perhaps technically helpful, but artistically, not much. Frederick L. Crane: in some spots labeled "Fred L. Crane" - "After The Ball - a romance": having no relation to the old standard "gay nineties" tune; a brief piano piece, showy but with little integrity in the melodic line, harmony, in essence - blasé; J. W. Crane "2 Romances Sans Paroles": published in 1877 by Hartmann in Paris, very much "à la Mendelsohn or J. Burgmüller"; again, nice but not "earth-shaking". There was an entry for Lucy Crane, who apparently was sister of the noted illustrator Walter Crane, - her contribution is entitled "Baby's Opera"; (my thought on seeing the title, one might have difficulty holding the attention of either the cast, the audience or both.) Upon a closer look I see that it is a collection of nursery rhymes put to melody, which melodies she ascribed to "great masters of the past", so she is in fact the editor of the collection accompanied by artistic images of her brother, the noted illustrator. That leaves us with one remaining composer: Helen C. Crane and the "one" oeuvre that is listed here: her "Piano Trio in E Major, op.20". One piece, three movements, about 60 printed pages total, published in Germany by Gustav Vetter in 1907. I quickly ran off a copy, and waited anxiously for some spare time to run through it.

Eventually the opportunity came, one hour before a choral rehearsal which I was directing. When I began playing through the music I was actually amazed: it was quite bold, rather forward thinking; perhaps post-Brahms-ian, as one would hope, adventurous in its interrelation of keys, soaring melodies wonderful orchestration with each part very much in keeping with the technical parameters of each instrument. It seemed to be loaded with nuance, deeper meaning and ideas that warranted further study and repeated listening. There was certainly nothing wrong with any of the facets of the work, it showed great attention to detail, correct in all musical parameters on its face. I enjoyed the piece, beginning to end.

Opus 20 implied there had to be at least 19 other pieces or groupings of various sizes and instrumentation perhaps, but where were they? Were they ever published? What became of them? My mind was abuzz with curiosity and in the ensuing days I began some intensive exploration, running google searches and more, and it was not long before I came across an interesting discovery: in doing a search for "Helen C. Crane composer" I was ushered to a "url" which detailed a bequest from a New York City family to the city's library of all their important documents. This collection according to what I was able to ascertain was the Alexander Crane family's personal correspondence and spanned a period of more than a century, from the early 1800's to about 1940. Apparently Alexander was a personage of some note in New York City, enough so to warrant gathering together all of his correspondence in the NY Public Library. Closer examination showed that he was a Wall Street lawyer, a commissioned officer in the Civil War, and there was some sort of diplomatic connections in Italy,...why would this search for Helen Crane have brought me here?

Scanning through the contents of the collection which included a listing of family members, I came across Helen Cornelia Crane. Come to find out Helen C. Crane was Alexander's daughter and gradually the pieces began to fall into place. Helen's materials were not located with this larger collection at the main library. Rather her materials were housed at the NYPL "Cullman Center" Library for the Performing Arts at 40 Lincoln Center Plaza. When I checked this particular library's Helen C. Crane Collection listing, I was shocked! It was all there*; everything, either in its original manuscript form or both manuscript and published form along with ephemera concerning performances, playbills, requests from the Library of Congress for copies of awarded pieces, notes concerning her publishing agreements and records of payment, etc. a veritable mother-lode of material.

The only exception being her "Elegy for Cello" op. 57 for which she was awarded a prize in 1918. The Library of Congress subsequently requested a copy for their records (1944). Helen, having passed away in 1930, her sister, Caroline Crane Marsh obliged the Library of Congress, gifting them with what would seem to have been the only copy of the work. Hence, that work is no longer in the NYPL collection.

She was born in 1868 the second child with four sisters and a brother. She must have been very talented and showed a keen interest in the study of music. She ended up a student of Xaver Scharwenka, a noted Polish pianist and composer, who was performing and teaching from NYC at that time. Xaver's brother, Philip was also a musician, a pianist, composer, and educator and was director of the Klindworth-Scharwenka Conservatory in Berlin, Germany. I can only surmise that having worked with Ms. Crane, Scharwenka, became aware of her gifts and abilities and potential. With a brother heading up a conservatory in Europe, perhaps that would be the logical continuation of her studies, at this Berlin Conservatory with his brother as her composition teacher.

According to the NYPL Performance Library division whose listings I was able to find online, there were somewhere in the vicinity of 4 cu. ft. of original and published manuscripts of Helen's writings. The list included notations as to the nature of its contents, the various opus numbers, methods of copy, pen, pencil or published. It looked as though everything was there, however the breadth of her output was a bit larger than 20: there are 74 numbered works. ...op. 74 being her last. Included in her output were two symphonies with sketches for a 3rd, several symphonic tone-poems, well over 200 works for piano, choral works, songs for solo voice, sonatas for violin, cello, a larger work for orchestra and chorus. It was amazing.

I soon made my way to NYC to get a first hand look at this Collection that was locked away in the archives and only available by appointment. It was amazing to see the extent of the collection neatly housed in seventeen archival boxes. The documents were in pristine condition, bearing no impression they had been even touched since the day the were donated. The Library made no claims to copyright and certainly the pieces were past statutory protection (all except op.74 composed before 1923). They could not let the documents be photocopied but there was no prohibition on available-light images taken with a camera or cellphone. Over the next year with three successive visits to NY I came away with some 3,440 images of Helen's own manuscripts.

In sharing this music with others, people have asked the obvious question: "with the same last name, are you related to her?" Well, it is an interesting question: Ellery Bicknell Crane in his 2 - volume set "The Cranes of Massachusetts" (pub. 1900) does a masterful job of tracing our family's ancestry back to the mid 17th century and to the immigration of a handful of Cranes who came to the New World. There were two brothers, Henry & Benjamin, and their father John Crane, who landed in Boston, and described themselves as being of "Muddy Brook" (generally the area around today's Boston University). The boys eventually moved once again to the Wethersfield colony on the Connecticut River. Another "Henry" Crane was located in the area of Milton, MA. He himself had a son and a grandson also named Benjamin, as if there might be some naming after, an uncle of ancestor, but there is at this time, no conclusive evidence.

Alexander Crane is descended from the Henry Crane of Milton, MA, I am descended from Benjamin Crane of Connecticut, son of John Crane, Muddy Brook or Boston, MA. If there is a connection it would be father of John and that would make Helen & myself eighth cousins, four times removed. But that matters little. The music is what matters and it is here and available, no longer sequestered away on a dusty library shelf. And the music speaks for itself.

Bernard Crane
arranger & editor

January, 2019

THE COMPOSER

Helen Cornelia Crane was born September 5, 1868, just a few short years after the end of the Civil War to Col. Alexander Baxter Crane, a native of Massachusetts and his young wife, Laura Cornelia Mitchell, a native of South Carolina. Col. Alexander Crane, a legal studies graduate of Amherst College was commissioned an officer on the side of the North and his young wife was daughter of the Wroughton Mitchell family of Charleston, South Carolina who for generations had lived in that part of the country. Certainly their relatives and acquaintances embraced both sides of the chasm that divided the nation. To this young couple was born Helen Cornelia, along with four other daughters and a son. Their earliest home was St. Mark's Place in New York's lower east side. Eventually Col. Crane's law career led to a flourishing Wall Street legal practice and they purchased property and built their permanent home in Scarsdale, NY.

She must have exhibited artistic talent at a young age since by her late teens she was embarked on studies in music in one of the most enviable of locations: Europe. She studied at the then "Klindworth-Scharwenka" Conservatory in Berlin. These studies culminated in her choice of composition as her major musical endeavor and she studied three years with noted composer and conservatory director Philipp Scharwenka. She was soon winning competitions and gaining much warranted recognition. German publishing houses recognized her work and she saw the publication of numerous of her pieces. Maintaining a regular home in Germany over the next couple of decades, she made several cross-Atlantic voyages for the sake of concertizing and teaching; one such trip in 1904 was for the purpose of hearing the Berlin Philharmonic perform her tone poem, *The Last Tournament* at the "World's Fair" that year, the *St. Louis Exposition*. She continued her intercontinental career until the fall of 1917 when the continued strife and turmoil of the First World War made it decidedly unsafe to continue.

At this time she returned to the her family home in Scarsdale, NY a place they affectionately nicknamed "Holmhurst" and here she remained for the most part; barring a few excursions & trip to Kaprun, Austria, where she traveled one last time "for the purpose of her health". Ultimately she passed away in November, 1930 in Scarsdale, NY and was laid to rest in the cemetery of St. James the Less Episcopal Church alongside her parents. She left behind her hand-written manuscripts in the care of her remaining siblings. Her youngest sister, Laura Vernon Crane Burgess ultimately donated this valuable trust to the New York Public Library, where the collection has been housed since the 1940's. Most of these pieces are there in their original manuscript form, showing the evolution of Ms. Crane's calligraphy and the blossoming of her musical art. Among this collection are over eighty works for the piano, several chamber works, orchestral tone poems such as *The Last Tournament*: her *Evangeline Overture*, *Cassandra* for female voice and orchestra, her *Serenade* for orchestra, two symphonies, *Psalm 42* for orchestra and chorus along with a multitude of song settings of various poets and pieces for organ. She was well noted in her day, lauded in various music periodicals of the time, even being listed in a compendium of composers in the United States, in *W.S.B Mathew's "A Popular History of The Art of Music..." (2nd edition 1906)*. But time is not always kind in its passing. Sometimes lives are dwarfed by events that overtake them in the memories of future generations. Bach was forgotten until Mendelssohn revived the memory of his music. And so it has been with Helen C. Crane. With this edition of her music hopefully our quiet sister speaks again. Let today's performers and today's listener be the judge. As a composer and as a music theorist, I do believe she warrants serious consideration. She stands as an integral part of the flowing forth of what is a truly "American" music, her life spanning that period of time between the Civil War and the "Great Depression", a time period known as the "Belle Époque", "the gilded age", a time shaken, rocked and irretrievably lost to an even greater war, World War I. Ms. Crane occupies a unique spot between late romanticism and the subsequent quest for new expression in music, enjoining her efforts to those of others, pushing the limits of tonality and yet retaining the memorable communication of which music is most capable.

Bernard Crane, editor
January 17, 2019

SELECTED ART SONGS OF

HELEN C. CRANE

MEDIUM VOICE

BOOK TWO

TABLE OF CONTENTS

I   Love Poems of Marie von Vorst op. 28

       1. In The Window .... p. 1
       2. Old Time Melody .... p. 7
       3. The Sign (#4 in set).. p. 10

II   Old English Songs op. 73

       1. Content *(Thomas Dekker)*..p. 15
       2. Pack Clouds Away *(Thomas Heywood)*..p. 20
       3. Song *(Wm. Shakespeare)*...p. 24
       4. Under The Greenwood Tree *(text of Wm. Shakespeare)*..p. 26
       5. The Passionate Shepherd To His Love *(Christopher Marlowe)*..................................p. 29
       6. O Sweet Delight *(Thomas Campion)* ....p. 35
       7. To Daffodils *(Robert Herrick)*..p. 39

III   Newer English Songs op. 74

       1. I Wandered Lonely As A Cloud *(Wm. Wordsworth)* ....p. 42
       2. *(not included)*
       3. A May Burden *(Francis Thompson)*..p. 46
       4. My Love Is Like A Red, Red Rose *(Robert Burns)*...p. 50
       5. A Garden Song *(Austin Dobson)*...p. 54
       6. Turn O' The Year *(Katherine Hinkson)*..p. 58
       7. April *(William Watson)*...p. 61
       8. The Fiddler of Dooney *(W. B. Yeats)* ....p. 63

In The Window

Helen C. Crane
Op. 28 no.1

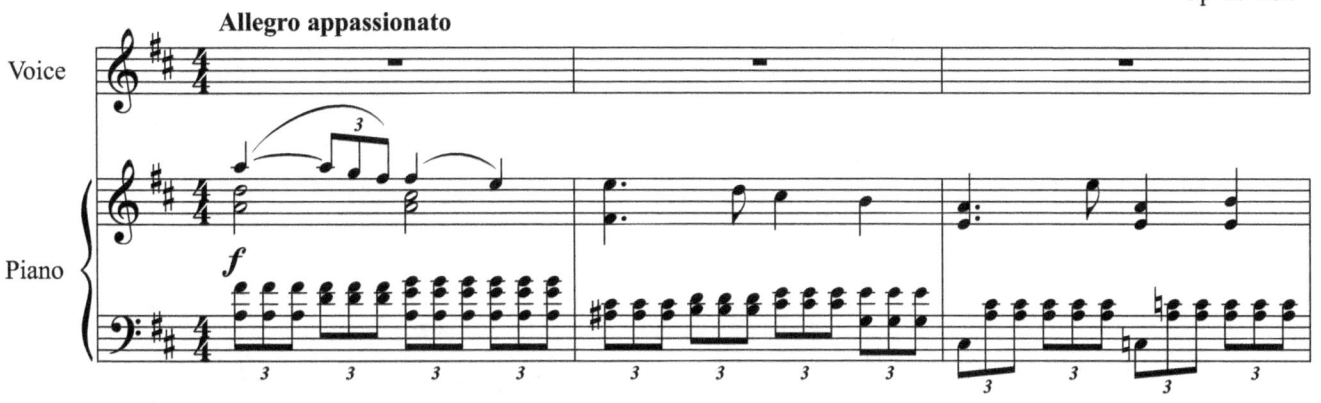

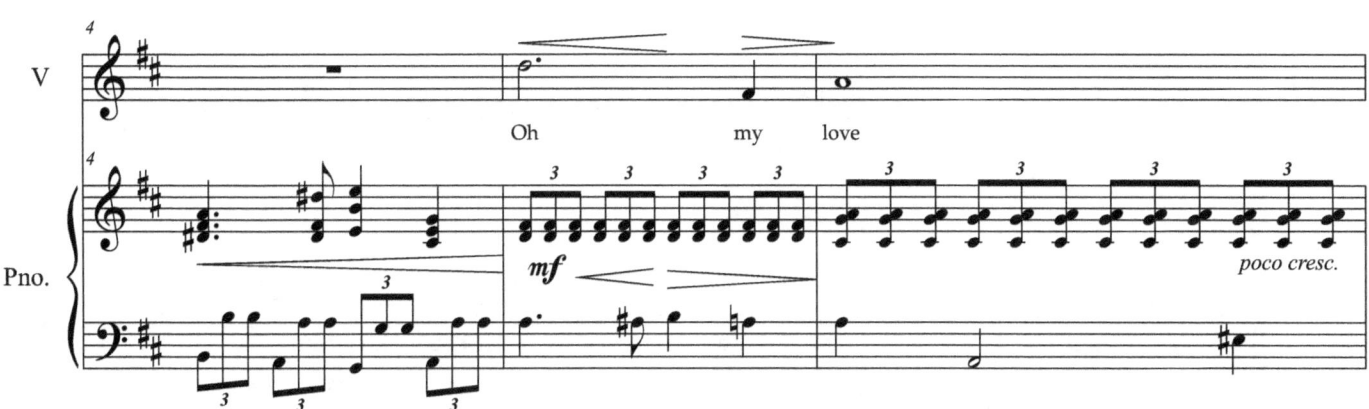

©2020 Bernard R. Crane
all rights reserved

Old Time Melody

Helen C. Crane
Op. 28, no. 2

©2020 Bernard R. Crane
all rights reserved

The Sign

Helen C. Crane
Op. 28, no. 4

©2020 Bernard R. Crane
all rights reserved

Old English Songs
Content

poem by Thomas Dekker

Helen C. Crane
Op. 73, no.1

©2020 Bernard R. Crane
all rights reserved

Old English Songs
Pack Clouds Away
poem by Thomas Heywood

Helen C. Crane
op.73, no. 2

©2020 Bernard R. Crane
all rights reserved

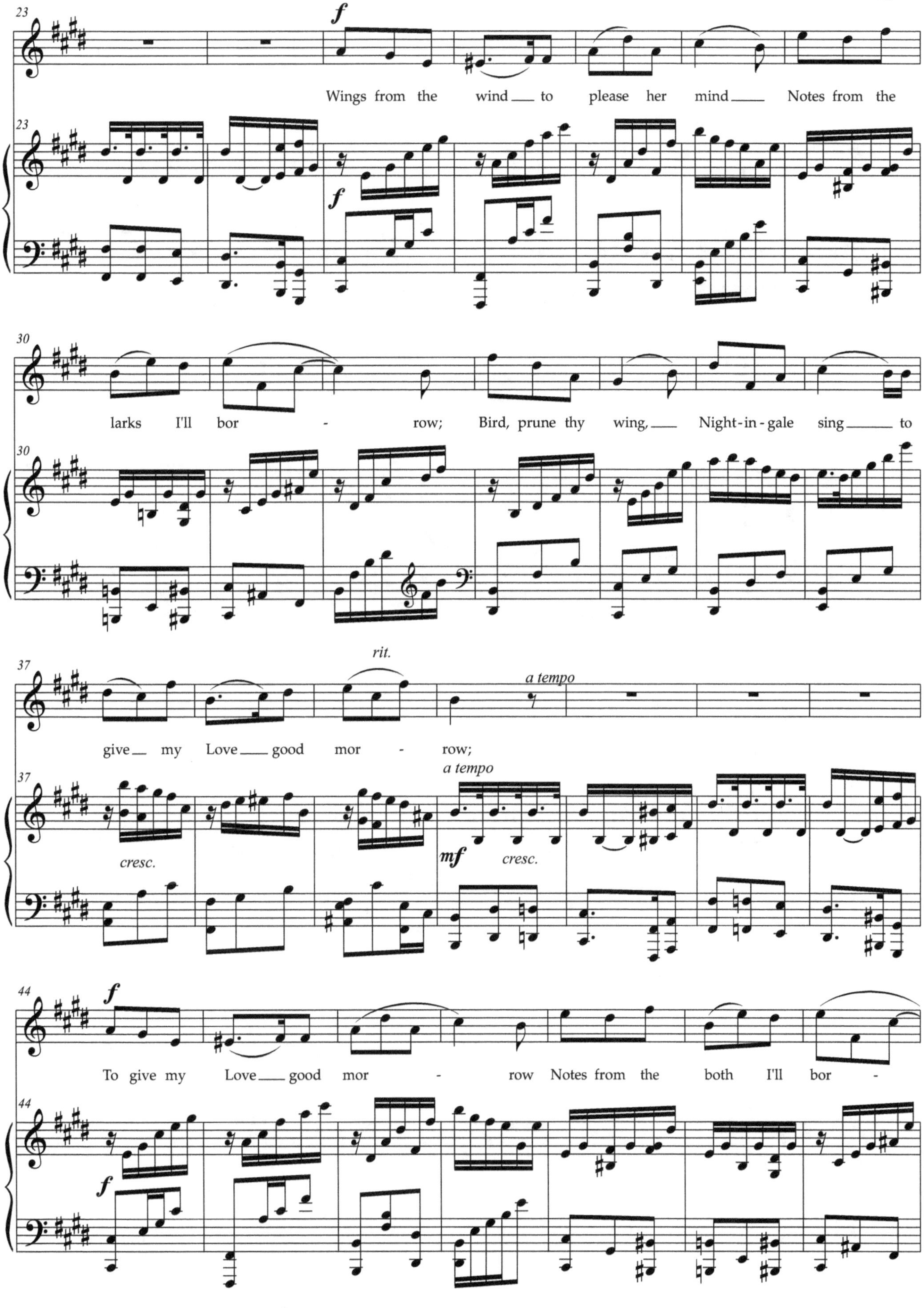
Pno.
Wings from the wind to please her mind Notes from the
larks I'll bor - row; Bird, prune thy wing, Night-in-gale sing to
rit.
a tempo
give my Love good mor - row;
a tempo
cresc.
cresc.
To give my Love good mor - row Notes from the both I'll bor -

Old English Songs
Song
text by William Shakespeare

Helen C. Crane
Op. 73, no.3

©2020 Bernard R Crane
all rights reserved

Old English Songs
Under The Greenwood Tree

poem by William Shakespeare

Helen C. Crane
Op. 73, no.4

©2020 Bernard R. Crane
all rights reserved

come ____ hi - ther, Here shall he see ____ no e - ne - my But win - ter and rough ____ wea - ther.

Old English Songs
The Passionate Shepherd To His Love

poem by Christopher Marlowe

Helen C. Crane
Op. 73, no. 5

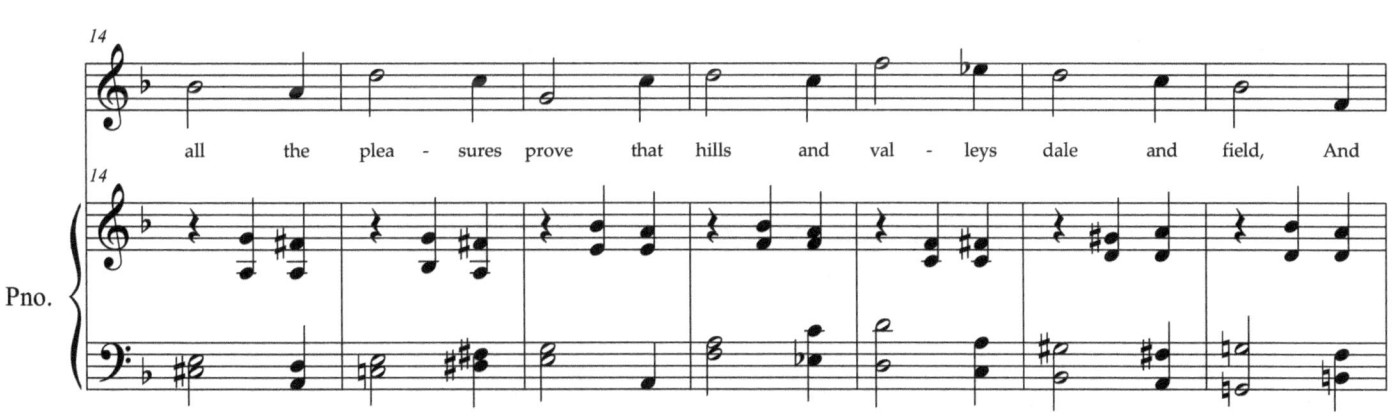

©2020 Bernard R. Crane
all rights reserved

Old English Songs
O Sweet Delight

poem by Thomas Campion

Helen C. Crane
Op.73, no.6

©2020 Bernard R. Crane
all rights reserved

Old English Songs
To Daffodils

poem by Robert Herrick

Helen C. Crane
Op. 73, no.7

©2020 Bernard R. Crane
all rights reserved

Newer English Songs
I Wandered Lonely As A Cloud

text by William Wordsworth

Helen C. Crane
Op. 74, no. 1

©2020 Bernard R. Crane
all rights reserved

46

Newer English Songs
A May Burden

poem by Francis Thompson

Helen C. Crane
Op. 74, no. 3

©2020 Bernard R. Crane
all rights reserved

Helen C. Crane — A May Burden — op.74, no.1

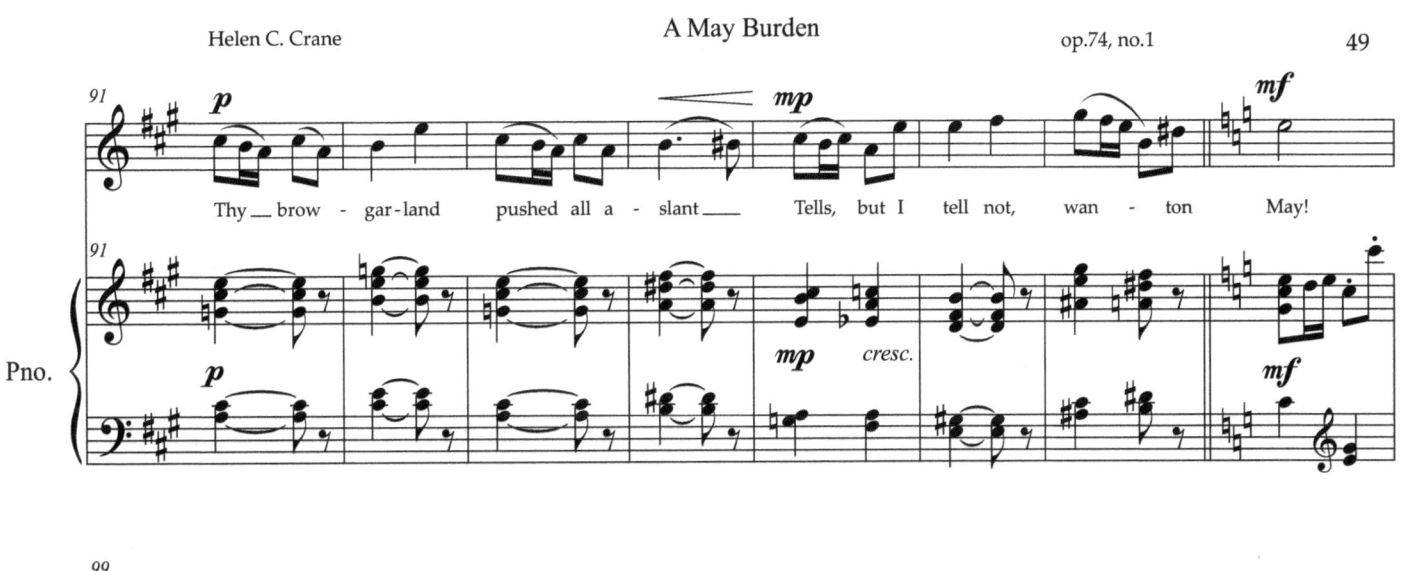

Newer English Songs
My Love Is Like A Red, Red Rose
text by Robert Burns

Helen C. Crane
Op. 74, no. 4

Newer English Songs

A Garden Song

poem by Austin Dobson

Helen C. Crane
Op. 74, no. 5

Here in this sequestered close Bloom the hyacinth and rose;

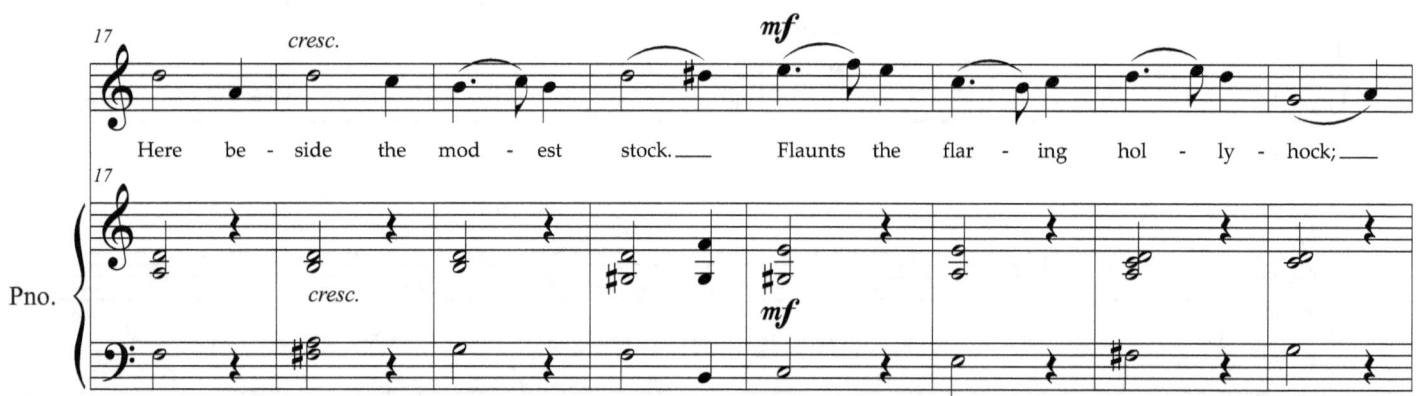

Here beside the modest stock Flaunts the flaring hollyhock;

* In Greek mythology Alcinous was King of the Phaesians and gave expensive gifts to Jason & the Argonauts.
** In Greek mythology the "Pierides" were the nine sisters who challenged the Muses in song, and were turned into birds.

©2020 Bernard R. Crane
all rights reserved

58

Newer English Songs
Turn O' The Year

poem by Katherine Hinkson

Helen C. Crane
Op. 74, no. 6

©2020 Bernard R. Crane
all rights reserved

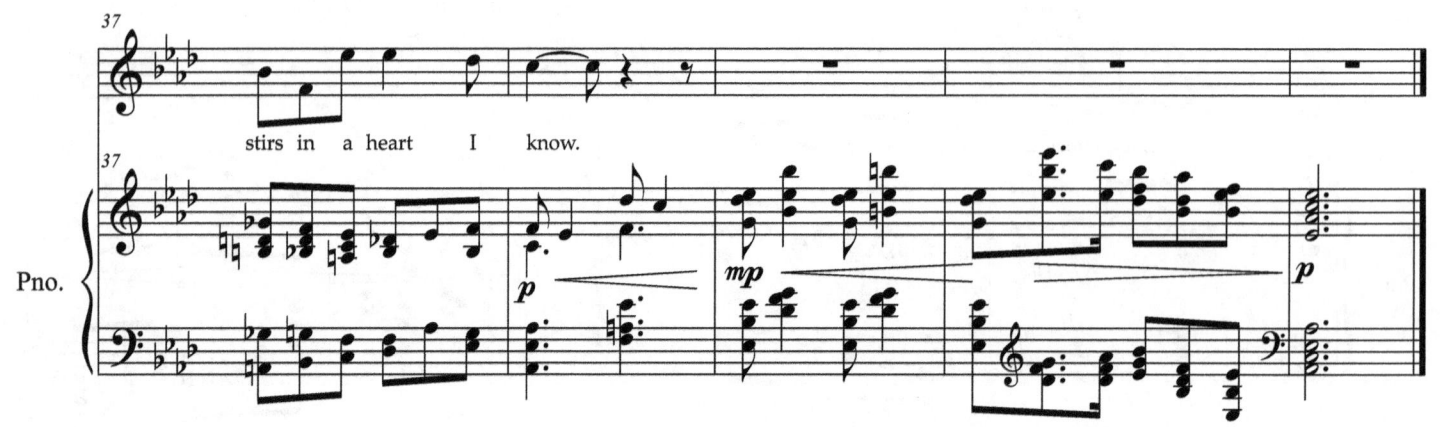

Newer English Songs
April
poem by William Watson

Helen C. Crane
Op. 74, no. 7

©2020 Bernard R. Crane
all rights reserved

Newer English Songs
The Fiddler Of Dooney

poem by William Butler Yeats

Helen C. Crane
Op. 74, no. 8

* In considering the tempo for this piece "allegro scherzando" (quick and joking) is more an indicator of mood than a tempo marking; the threshold of " allegro " being about dotted quarter to 109. If the dotted quarter is 109 it seems to fast for the iteration of the text; dotted quarter = 75 thru 90 seems about right; the piece might be better labeled "Andante scherzando" BC

©2020 Bernard R. Crane
all rights reserved

www.ingramcontent.com/pod-product-compliance
Lightning Source LLC
LaVergne TN
LVHW061343060426
835512LV00016B/2647